Thomas Christy

Christy's cyclopedia

How to do everything and how everything is done

Thomas Christy

Christy's cyclopedia
How to do everything and how everything is done

ISBN/EAN: 9783337224523

Printed in Europe, USA, Canada, Australia, Japan

Cover: Foto ©Lupo / pixelio.de

More available books at **www.hansebooks.com**

CHRISTY'S CYCLOPEDIA

OR

HOW TO DO EVERYTHING,

AND

HOW EVERYTHING IS DONE.

Containing the most Valuable Information on all subjects of interest, with about one hundred and fifty of the Best

RECEIPTS AND PRESCRIPTIONS

EVER BEFORE PUBLISHED.

JUST WHAT EVERYBODY NEEDS AND WANTS.

Knowledge that has Cost the Author Thousands of Dollars by experience and otherwise.

A KEEP SAKE FOR EVERY FAMILY.

SEE CONTENTS.

PRICE ONE DOLLAR.

PUBLISHED BY THE AUTHOR,

T. J. CHRISTY, Olney, Ills.

1871.

Printed by O. T. Beck, Journal Office.

PREFACE.

In presenting this work to the Public, I feel confident that it will be thankfully received, and appreciated by all who peruse its pages. Never before has so much valuable information been published in so small a work; it contains all new and valuable discoveries of the age, together with all Secrets and Receipts of all professions and businesses. There are several Receipts in this little book, that are worth ten times its weight in gold, and no family should be without them. My desire is to give the public the benefit of all my knowledge, and experience of several years of traveling through about sixteen States in the Union, and in mingling and dealing with all kinds and classes of people. Several times I have paid extravagent prices to obtain some mans secret of doing or cureing something.

And whereas the public is being continually imposed on, I propose to furnish them with a ready adviser upon all subjects, and which will save them dollars upon dollars, if goverened by its dictates.

It tells you how all kinds of valuable remedies are made. It tells you how all kinds of Soaps are made. It tells the secrets of all professions and trades. It tells just what every body wants to know.

This book will be mailed free to any address in the U. S. on receipt of price, One Dollar, by addressing

T. J. CHRISTY, Olney, Illinois.

AUTHOR AND PUBLISHER.

1871.

CONTENTS.

PAGE.

Ague Pill..17
Ague to cure without quinine....................................17
Asthma to cure...11
Burns to cure..16
Boils to cure..26
Burns and scalds to cure..24
Blacking water proof...27
Blacking for metal founders......................................22
Bunions to cure...18
Butter how to keep..39
Blueing liquid for clothes..42
Breaking horses...42
Big shoulder in horses..48
Blind stagers in hogs to cure.....................................51
Bots in horses to cure..49
Biscuits how to make excellent..................................38
Balm of beauty how to make.....................................35
Cement for iron...26
Cement for iron and stone...23
Cement for metal and glass..23
Cement Diamond...23
Corns and warts to remove.......................................20
Corn salve...20
Catarrh to cure...18
Cosmetic solution...16
Colic in children...15
Colic in horses...46&49
Cholera and cholera infantum.....................................9
Cough syrup..11
Cough tonic...11
Cancer to cure..12
Cancer symptoms...12
Cholera morbus..15
Cocoa-nut Cake..37
Cocoa-nut pie...37
Cake favorite...37
Coughs in horses..45
Corns in horses..45
Coughs in horses..45
Cramp in horses...46
Chow-chow to make..35
Cologne how to make the best....................................32
Dysentery to cure..14
Diarrhea when accompanied with water discharges.........15
Diarrhea when accompanied with pain.........................26
Diptheria...16
Dye for the hair..29
Dyeing carpet warp, green, purple, yellow, and pink......36

CONTENTS.

Dye for woolen crimson and scarlet............................36
Dyes red...37
Distemper in horses to cure..................................46
Eyes a valuable remedy for...................................10
Eggs how to keep...39
Eggs to preserve...38
Flux to cure...14
Fits to cure...17
Frosted feet and salve to cure...............................18
Felons to cure...24
Fluid for writing and coppying...............................27
Feathers to clean..35
Foot evil and fistula to cure................................48
Founder in horses to cure.................................48&49
Flies to keep from horses....................................46
Glue liquid..23
Gingerbread how to make......................................38
Glanders in horses...49
German puffs the best way to make............................37
Hair to dye..29
Hair to grow soft and glossy.................................34
Hair how to color..35
Hair restorative...30
How four ponds of butter is made from one gallon of milk.42
Horses to break..42
Hide bound how to treat......................................45
Hog cholera to cure..50
Horses the end of...50
Horses to get out of fire....................................49
Hooks in horses to cure......................................49
Honey artificial how to make.................................32
Ink coppying and all other kinds..........................28&29
Inflamation of the eye in horses.............................46
King of pain or ready relief.................................10
Linament corosive..46
Liquid bluing for clothing...................................42
Mucilage how to make...29
Meat how to preserve...32
Milk to preserve...51
Neuralgia to cure..17
Neuralgia toothache or carial relieved.......................25
Ointment spermacetic to make.................................22
Oil macassar for hair..20
Oil star hair..30
Omlette soufle to make.......................................38
Pencil marks to fix on paper.................................33
Poison for bugs...20&27

CONTENTS.

Plating silver how done................................26
Pains to remove................................10
Piles internal and external................................18
Plaster sticking or court................................19
Paint cheap white house how to make................................39
Pudding how to make................................38
Plaster for corns................................19
Plating without a battery................................21
Plating on iron or steel................................22
Plaster Paris how to mix to prevent drying too fast.......23
Pain killer magnetic................................25
Rheumatism a sure cure for................................9
Rheumatism speedy cure for................................25
Ring bone treatment for................................45
Rusk how to make................................38
Rolls to make fine and delicious................................37
Small pox and sea sickness to cure 32
Sea sickness curable................................21
Summer complaint how to cure................................10
Snake bites to cure................................20
Salve for sore lips and scalds and burns to cure...........24
Silver solution for plating................................26
Silver wash how to make................................30
Soap of all kinds how to make........................40&41
Spavin bone to cure................................43&44
Strains and sore tongue in horses to cure 45
Shaving cream how to make................................30
Tape worm how to remove................................16
Tooth drops how to make................................25
Tooth paste how to make................................26
Transferring engravings................................31
Transfer on Plaster Paris................................32
Varnish for iron work................................30
Vinegar how to make................................41&50
Vinegar how to make out of cider........................51
Wen how to cure................................20
Wines how to make................................33
Whiskers forced to grow................................34
Washing fluid how to make................................41
Washing compound how to make very good............39

How to sell Patents.

In order to sell County and State rights on any improvement, you must first show up the merits of your invention by demonstration, then you must prove to the satisfaction of your customer to whom you are trying to sell a State or County right, that he can make money by investing, from the fact that you have the best thing in that line and that it sells readily at a fair profit; this you can do by making a thorough canvas of some town or county, selling and getting as many orders as you possibly can for the machine upon which you have an improvement; and in so doing you convince the public that money can be made out of your invention with energy and industry, without which all inventions and improvements are a failure; never start out telling everybody that you have a patent that you want to sell; never make use of the term patent right, but always speak of your invention as a valuable improvement; if it is a plough say plough, if it is a wagon say wagon, or whatever it is, call it by its proper name, endeavor to make the impression that you have got a good and valuable improvement, and that you are doing a fair, honorable and legitimate business, and if you have what you claim you claim you have, you will have no difficulty in disposing of terrritory at reasonable rates. Some men more especially patentees make a very sad mistake by asking too much for State and County rights. Sell cheap and sell fast; a man had better close out the United States in a few months time at an average of from five to ten dollars per county, than to sell a State or few Counties at an enormous price, then let the thing die on his hands, from the fact that the parties to whom he has made a sale report the thing a swindle and a humbug for the reason that they have paid more money for the teritory than they can possibly realize even by a close and energetic canvas of their territory; by this means they become discouraged and conclude that they are swindled, and so they report it, although the transaction and sale was made perfectly fair and honorable. Now the report goes about that you have a humbug, and that you are swindling the public with it. Whilst if a sale was made at low and reasonable rates the parties would go to work and make money and report favorable and advertise your invention, and would be the means of your selling a great deal more territory, and as soon as they had canvassed and disposed of what they had purchased return and purchase again, and soon you would gain the confidence of the public; and everybody would be running after you to buy territory, because now it is a demonstrated fact that everybody is making money out of it, and soon a small fortune will be realized. There are some classes of invention that a man never ought to offer to sell territory on; such articles as would come under the head of merchandise, that can be manufactured, shipped and transported for less money than they could be got up for all through the country. On these class of improvements you should either sell the entire patent out to some company or have it manufactured on a royalty and put it into the market the same as Ploughs, Reapers, Mowers, etc., for whenever you propose to sell State and County rights on such inventions and improvements, you virtually prove to the public that you have a humbug and that there is no protection in it for the claims on it as secured are not worth a fig, from the fact they could not be used without infringing on a half dozen other inventors or more.

Caution to the Public.

I would here caution all persons who are about to purchase territory on some patent, to be very careful in examining the claims to see that they are good and that the machine as constructed does not infringe upon the claims of other inventors, for the value of an improvement consists in its protection as well as its merits, for a patent that infringes on the rights of others is worthless, without license has been obtained from the infringed parties, to manufacture, vend and use the same. A man runs just as much risk in buying territory on a patent without first making a thorough investigation of its protection and claims, as he would in buying a farm and paying for it without examining the records, to see that there are no mortgages or loans against it. Never buy a patent unless you are certain that it does not infringe upon other mens rights, and this you cannot positively know without an investigation at the Patent Office.

Never buy a patent because some friend, neighbor or acquaintance advises you to do so, for as general thing they are interested in getting a part of your money; many times a man gets sold out by his pretended friends, as a general thing the seller divides with those kind of friends. I never knew a man to go around among his neighbors and advise them to buy a patent right or even recommended it highly unless he was interested in getting a portion of the proceeds realized from the sales.

Worthless patents are generally sold by neighbor helping sell neighbor. What I mean by that is this; one neighbor will go to another and insist on him going his havers in buying a State or counties as the case may be and if he succeeds in getting his neighbor to join him as a general thing he gets his half for nothing and a portion of the money that his patner has paid.

Now my readers I would advise you never to go into partnership with any man in buying a patent, if you cannot buy one on your one hook let it alone, never buy on the judgment of others, for if you are not qualified to deal on your own judgment you had better let it alone. No man ever got rich a speculating when controlled and governed by the opinions and notions of others; it is well enough for a man to listen to and learn all he can, but never invest money unless you do it on your own judgment especially in patent rights. Whenever a person proposes to sell you a county or State on some patent right and begins to figure and explain to you how you can make a small fortune in a very short time, just ask him to please explain to you how it is and why he don't want to make that money himself, and that you do not know of any person that is any better qualified to do so than himself, and you will soon find him hunting for another customer, for the facts are this as a general rule to which there may be a few exceptions; a man never will go around through the country peddling out patent righths on a patent that is of any value, for if it is a good and valuable improvement, there is no necessity for so doing, for if he is not able to manufacture and introduce the article himself, there are a plenty of firms and companies that will do so and pay him a fair royalty on it.

A Sure Cure for Rheumatism.

There are a large number of living witnesses who can testify to the merits of the following prescription, which was handed to me by Mr. Jones, of Olney, Ills., who may be addressed as to its merits; as it has been retained as a family secret for years, he desires that the afflcted public may be relieved by its publication. Saltpeter 1 drachm, pulverizen Opium 2 grains; mix and devide into four powders, take one powder every four hours in a little cold tea, if necessary double the dose and repeat until relieved.

Here is another remedy that is highly recommended for Rheumatism. One oz Spirits Turpentine, one oz Cayenne Pepper, one oz Oil Sassafras, one oz Oil Hemlock, one oz Oil Organum. Put all into one quart of Alcahol; shake well before taking. Dose, one good swallow before meals, three times per day.

Rheumatic Liniment.

Take oil of linseed, oil of cedar, and oil of Amber, of each 1 oz; Gum Champhor 1-2 oz, dissolve in 1-2 oz of Sweet oil, by rubbing in a mortar, first adding to the Champhor a few drops of Alcohol, so as to powder it; Spirits Turpentine and Laudanum, each 1-2 oz; mix and shake well. Rub the parts affected thoroughly.

The Best Remedy Known for Cholera and Cholera Infantum.

1 oz Laudnam, 1 oz Spirits of Camphor, 2 oz Tincture of Ginger, 2 oz Capsicum. Dose for adult, teaspoonfull in a wine glass of water

I think the above will be improved by adding about four drachms of Chloroform. Every family should always keep the above in the house; it would save them many a dollar and sometimes life. Very often in those cases, the Physician gets there too late.

A tea made of Vervain root is a sure relief for Colic, persons subject to colic will use this tea every day for several weeks will never have it again.

A Valuable Remedy for Sore Eyes.

This remedy will never fail if used in time. 1-2 oz Sulphate Zinc, 1-2 oz White Copperas, 1-2 teaspoonfull of Laudanum, 1 pint of rain water. Make strong enough to feel the burning a little for about an hour after using. Bathe the eyes twice or three times per day, until the inflamation is gone. I have known the above eye water to cure some very sore eyes, with two or three applications.

In old standing cases of ulcerated or granulated sore eyes, it is sometimes necessary to use in connection with the eyewater, a little caustic, by turning the eyelids up and blow in with a goosquill. Bathe the temples with Iodine. In bad cases, take pine gum, plaster it on a cloth, drop two or three drops of Croten Oil on it, and apply to the back of the neck, let it remain until slightly blistered; bathe the eyes night and morning with warm soft water. Use light diet, and keep bowels regular. Eat no grease.

I paid $75 for the above to a Physician, who was noted for his success.

McBride's Eclectric Relief, or King of Pain.

I obtained this from a gentleman in Kansas, he says he paid $500 for the receipt. 1-2 galen Alcohol, 8 oz Aqua Ammonia, 4 oz Oil Organum, 2 oz Oil Cedar, 2 oz Oil Sassafras, 3 oz No. Six, 3 oz Chloroform, 1-2 oz Oil Annis, 1 oz Oil Hemlock; then take 10 live Bees, put them into a pint of soft water and boil down to one gill and add to the above. Shake well and you will have what McBride made $40,000 with in St. Louis, and about as much or more in every city.

I have tested the above and find it just as good as any relief known, for all kinds of aches and pains, it is a very useful medicine to keep in the house; it will do all that any of those quick reliefs will do.

Remedy for Diarrhea and Summer Complaint.

1 teaspoonful best Rhubarb, 1 oz Cinnamon or Nutmeg; steep in half pint of water, when cold strain and add 1 tea spoonfull soda, 1 tea spoonfull Essence Peppermint, 2 teaspoonsfull best Brandy, and sweeten with loaf sugar to suit

the taste. Dose, one tablespoonfull, repeat as often as the bowels moves, until they are checked.

The above is highly recommended by families who have used it for years.

Cough Syrup.

Syrup of Squills, 2 oz, Tartarized Antimony, 8 grains Sulphate of Morphine 5 grains, pulverized Gum Arabic 1-4 oz, Honey 1 oz, Water 1 oz; mix. Dose for an adult, 1 small teaspoonful, repeat in half an hour if it does not relieve. Child in proportion.

ANOTHER COUGH SYRUP.—Put 1 quart Hoarhound for 1 quart water, and boil it down to a pint, and 2 or 3 sticks of Liquorice and a tablespoonful of essence of Lemon. Take a teaspoonful three times a day, or as often as the cough may be troublesome. This receipt has been sold for $100.

COUGH TONIC.—1 quart of Rye Whiskey, 1 quart of strained Honey, 2 oz Pine Gum, mix the whiskey and gum together in one bottle, and put the honey in another, and cork them air tight, put them into a kettle of cold water and boil them a few minutes, then take out and put them together. Dose teaspoonful three times a day.

The above is highly recommended.

To Cure Asthma.

Take Elecampane, angelica, comfrey, and spikenard roots, with hoarhound tops, of each 1 oz; bruise and steep in honey 1 pint. Dose, a tablespoonful, taken hot every few minutes, until relief is obtained, then several times daily until a cure is affected.

The above is recommended as a sure cure. It is also an excellent remedy for all kinds of coughs.

ANOTHER CURE.—Oil of tar 1 dr; tincture of veratrum viride 2 dr; simple syrup 2 drs; mix. Dose for adults 15 drops, 3 or 4 times daily.

This is highly recommended.

Cancers to Cure.

Everything is not a cancer that is called cancer, A good many of our cancer Doctors who have gained a little notoriety in curing a few old sores, pronounce everything cancer. I was told of a gentleman a short time ago, that was advised to go and see a cancer doctor; as he had what was supposed to be a cancer on the jaw. Accrdingly he called on the old doctor who told him that he had a cancer sure enough, and he would cure it for one hundred dollars; fifty cash in hand, and fifty when the cure was affected. As he was short for money he could not comply with the doctors terms, and went away thinking he would make some arrangements to raise the money. After some consideration he concluded to call and see another doctor; who made no pretention as a cancer doctor, but he was a good practicing Physician, he told him that he had no cancer, and to step with him into a dentist's office, which was close by; the dentist examined his jaw and found that there was a root of an old tooth in the jaw; which was the cause of the so-called cancer, and in a few minutes he extracted the tooth, and cured the cancer for fifty cents. And now my reader, my desire is to benefit, and save you money, by cautioning you against the impositions that are practiced all over the country. I now will proceed to give the best known remedy for cancers, and if you are governed by the instruction you can cure a cancer just as well as any cancer doctor in the U. S. for I give you what they concede to be the best known remedy.

CANCER SYMPTOMS.—A tumer surrounded with enlarged veins, it is also very painful, the skin being sometimes discolored and puckered. The whole tumer is particularly heavy, and at last breaks into a malignant ulcer, or sore, whose edges are raised, raged, uneven, and curl like the leaves of a flower; white streaks or bands cross it from the center to the cercumference, accompanyed with acute and darting pains. To relieve the pain, Opium may be taken in large doses. The sore should be defended from the air, by some mild ointment. Powdered chalk, scraped carrots, fresh hemlook leaves and powdered charcoal may be used for the same purpose.

Cancer, How to Cure.

Red clover is said to be the latest and most valuable dis-
covery for the cure of cancer. Take the roots of red clover
and boil them down to a strong tea, then take some of the
tea and boil down as thick as you well can; then put it into
a puter dish and set it in the sun until it evaperates and
thickens up to about the consistency of honey; now let the
patient drink of the tea about three times per day, before
meals, and at the same time use the thickened compound on
the cancer, as follows: Never apply any medicine directly
on the raw sore, but commence applying the remedy all
around the sore part of the cancer, as far out as the flesh
seems to be affected, untill the roots of the cancer are killed;
and this you will know by the sore gradualy drying up, then
commence applying the remedy to the sore and still continue to apply all around and over the sore, until it is entirely dried and healed up, using of the tea as before stated
all the while.

Another Process Recommended for the Cure of Cancer.

Ashes of red-oak bark, boiled down to the consistency of
molasses, and cover the cancer with it, in about an hour
afterward, cover it with a plaster of tar, which must be removed after a few days; and if any partuberance remain in
the wound, apply more potash and the plaster again until
this shall disappear.

Another remedy as given by an old doctor in Ohio, who
has retired on a fortune realized from his curing cancers, which is as follows: Take a dozen or so of copper
cents, and put them into about half gallon of strong vinegar
let remain about 24 hours, then take out and separate the
verdigris from the vinegar, and apply the verdigris all
around and over the cancer until cured; washing and dressing once a day with castile soap.

I know several persons cured of cancer by application of
what is commonly known as sheep-sorel, an herb that generally grows around in the fence corners; you take this herb
and beet it up and get the juice all out, and put in a puter

dish, set it in the sun until it thickens up like molasses, then apply as you would other remedies.

This preparation never fails to cure Pole evil, or Fistula.

ANOTHER REMEDY, AS GIVEN BY DR. CHASE.—Take red oak bark ashes. 1 peck; put on them boiling water 6 quarts; let it stand 12 hours; then draw off the ley and boil to a thick salve; spread this pretty thick, upon a thick cloth, a little larger than the cancer, and let it remain on three hours, if it is too severe, half of that time; the same day, or the next, apply again three hours, which will generally effect a cure; after the last plaster, wash the sore with warm milk and water; then apply a healing salve made cf mutton tallow, bark of elder, with a little rosin and beeswax, (some of white lilly may be added,) stewed over a slow fire; when the sore begins to matter, wash it three or four times daily, renewing the savle each time; avoid strong diet, and strong drink, but drink a tea of sassafras root and spicewood tops, for a week before and after the plaster.

A Gentleman informs me that he has effectually cured himself of an obstinate cancer, "by the free use of potash," made from the ashes of red-oak, boiled to the consistency of molasses, used as a poultice, covering the whole with a coat of tar. Two or three applications will remove all protuberances; after which it is only necessary to heal the wound with common salve.

Cure for Flux and Dysentary.

Gum opium, 1 oz; gum kino 1 dr; gum camphor 40 grs; powdered nutmeg 1-2 oz; french brandy, jamacia spirits, 1 pint; color with cochineal or saffron. Before taking, cleans the bowels with caster oil. For a grown person 20 to 40 drops, three or four times a day. For children four to six drops; administer in a little mint tea, in which is mixed as much prepared chalk as will lie on the point of a teaspoon.

This is the remedy known for dysentary, and sells at retail for $1,00 per bottle.

CURE FOR DYSENTERY.—Take new churned Butter, before it is washed or salted, clarify over the fire, and skim off the milky particles; add 1-4 Brandy to preserve it, and loaf Sugar to sweeten; let the patient if an adult, take two table-spoonsful twice a day. The above is a sure cure, and is sold at a great profit.

Croup is often cured by giving Urine and Molasses, equal quantities. Goose oil is sometimes used instead of Molasses. Dose, from a tea to a tablespoonful of the mixture, according to age, repeat every fifteen minutes, if first does not vomit in that time.

Simple, but Effectual Remedy for Cholera Morbus.

Take the yellow of one egg, beat it up well and mix in one teaspoonful of black pepper. Dose, teaspoonful of mixture, after each operation until relieved.

I obtained this of Mr. Wilkerson of Olney, he says he has known it in use in his and other families for the last fifteen years, and has never known it to fail giving relief.

For children that has the summer complaint or diarrhea; parched flour will relieve them, and sometimes cures when nothing else will; feed it to them any way you can get them to eat it.

COLIC IN CHILDREN.—Give a scruple of powdered anis seed in their meat, or a small dose of magnesia; or a drachm of anisated tincture of rhubarb every three hours till it operates.

AROMATIC SYRUP OF RHUBARB.—Or as commonly known, "spiced syrup of rhubarb," much employed in summer complaints in infants and children. The dose for an infant is from half to a tea-spoonful, repeated every two hours till the passages indicate, by their color, that the medicine has operated.

FOR DIARRHEA, When accompanied by watery discharges. Take 4 ounces chalk-mixture, 1 ounce tincture kino, 1 ounce tincture catechu, 2 drachms laudanum.

Dose, one tablespoonful for an adult, after every thin stool.

Take pumpkin seeds six hundred, sugar one hundred grains, ethereal extract of male fern, sixty grains; water five fluid ounces; bruise the seed in a marble mortar with the sugar, add a fluid ounce of water, and when a homogeneous paste has been obtained add the extract of fern, and gradually mix in the rest of the water. The emulsion should be taken without straining, early in the morning in four doses at intervals of fifteen minutes; the bottle being well shaken each time. Two hours after, take a heavy dose of oil.

ANOTHER SIMPLE BUT EFFECTUAL REMEDY.—Take a pint of Pumpkin seeds and clean the outward shell off and pulverise or beat them up, then add half ounce of male fern root powdered finely, when that can't be had, the extract will answer, mix all together, and eat as you would mush. It is best for the patient to do without eating from twelve to twenty-four hours before taking the mixture. It should be taken in the morning on empty stomach, and in two hours afterward take a heavy dose of oil or some good and effective purgative, then look out for the worm. Care should be taken while at the stool not to break the worm into before it is entirely past. It is best for the patient to take a purgative the day before you take the worm remedy.

CURE FOR BURNS.—The whites of eggs have proved of late the most efficacious remedy for burns. Seven or eight successive applications soothes the pain and effectually excludes the burned parts from the air, and will be found fra preferable to collodion or cotton.

COSMETIC LOTION, SIMILAR TO PALMEY's.—Corrosive sublimate 1 gr; oil lavender half drachm; caster-oil one drachm; alcohol two ounces.

This preparation has a great reputation for the cure of tetter and for eruptions on the skin. Care should be used, in its application, not to let it get into the eyes or mouth.

To Cure Diptheria.

Take a common tobacco pipe, place a live coal in the bowl, drop a little tar upon the coal, draw the smoke into the mouth, and discharge it through the nostrils.

Lemon juice in diptheria; gargled in the throat, and swallow a little, is recommended as a sure cure.

From the french hospital.

Positive Cure for Ague without Quinine.

Peruvian bark, 2 oz, wild cherry tree bark 1 oz, cinnamon 1 dr, capsicum 1 teaspoonful, sulphur 1 oz, port wine 2 qts; let it stand two days. Buy your peruvian bark and pulverize it yourself, as it is often adulterated otherwise. Dose, one wine glassful every two or three hours after fever is off, then two or three per day till all is used; a certain cure.

Before taking the above, cleans the bowels with a dose of epsom salts, or other purgative.

ANOTHER SURE CURE.— Take pulverised galangal root 1 pound and put it in one gallon of alcohol. When the chill comes on bathe the feet in warm water; go to bed and cover up, and take a tablespoonful every fifteen minutes till the chill goes off; you will only have to take about three doses and you won't have any more chills. This never fails.

I am informed that our ex-county clerk, Mr. Johnson, while returning home from the army, obtained a simple but never failing remedy for ague, which he says he has tested, and never known it to fail. Made as follows : Take corn husks and boil down to a strong tea, and drink freely of it when the fever is off, or whenever you have any symptoms of a chill.

AGUE PILLS.-Extract cornis florida 40 grs; piperine, 20 grs; quinine 20 grs; make into 20 pills.

Sold at enormous profits.

Facial Neuralgia.

The following is an excellent preparation for facial neuralgia. Take chloroiorm two drachms, tincture cinchona two ounces, water two ounces; mix. Take a desertspoonful every three or hours four hours until the pain ceases. This preparation will relieve nervous headache.

An exclusive milk diet, without any solid food will cure epileptic fits.

Frosted Feet.

To relieve the intense itching of frosted feet, dissolve a lump of alum in a little water, and bathe the part with it, warming it before the fire. One or two applications are sure to give relief.

SALVE FOR FROST BITES.—Long known and highly valued in Germany.—Twenty-four ounces mutton tallow, twenty-four ounces hogs lard, four ounces peroxide iron, four ounces venice turpentine, two ounces oil bergamont, two ounces bole armenia, rubbed to a paste with olive oil. Melt together the tallow, lard, and peroxide of iron, stirring constantly until the mass assumes a perfectly black color; then add gradually the other ingredients, stirring until well mixed. Spread on linen, and apply daily. Its effect upon even the most painful frost sores is most extraordinary, and will, doubtless, be found equally beneficial in other sores.

Ointment for External Piles.

Stramonium ointment, half an ounce; ointment of galls half an ounce; sulphate morphine ten grains; make ointment. Apply night and morning.

BOLUS FOR INTERNAL PILES.—Powdered castile soap one ounce; powdered muriate ammonia, one ounce; powdered jalapa, one ounce; balsam copabia, sufficient to make into bolus. Insert one every night.

To CURE BUNIONS.—Bunions are usually hard to cure, but the following receipt has proved efficacious in many cases. Make an ointment of half an ounce of spermaceti and twelve grains of iodine, and apply twice or three times a day.

Catarrh.

Catarrh in the head can be cured by inhaling the smoke of muriate of ammonia, four of five times a day.

Twenty-five drops of tincture of lobelia, and two grs of the sulphate of quinine, taken four times a day, will cure the asthma.

Sticking, or Court Plaster.

This plaster is well known from its general use and its healing properties. It is merely a kind of varnished silk, and its manufactory is very easy.

Bruise a sufficient quantity of isinglass, and let it soak in a little warm water for four-and-twenty hours; expose it to heat over the fire till the greater part of the water is dissipated, and supply its place by proof spirits of wine, which will combine with the isinglass. Strain the whole through a piece of open linen, taking care that the consistence of the mixture shall be such that, when cool, it may form a trembling jelly.

Extend the piece of black silk, of which you propose making your plaster, on a wooden frame, and fix it in that position by means of tacks or pack-thread. Then apply the isinglass (after it has been rendered liquid by a gentle heat) to the skin with a brush of fine hair(badgers' is the best). As soon as this first coating is dried, which will not be long, apply a second; and afterwards, if you wish the article to be very superior, a third. When the whole is dry, cover it with two or three coatings of the balsam of Peru.

This is the genuine court plaster. It is pliable and never breaks, which is far from being the case with many of the spurious articles which are sold under that name. Indeed, this commodity is very frequently adulterated. A kind of plaster, with a very thick and brittle covering, is often sold for it. The manufacturers of this, instead of isinglass, use common glue, which is much cheaper; and cover the whole with spirit varnish, instead of balsam of Peru. This plaster cracks, and has none of the balsamic smell by which the genuine court plaster is distinguished. Another method of detecting the adulteration is to moisten it with your tongue on the side opposit to that which is varnished; and, if the the plaster be genuine, it will adhere exceedingly well. The adulterated plaster is too hard for this; it will not stick, unless you moisten it on the varnish side.—The Painter, Gilbert, and Varnisher's Companion.

Corn Plaster.

Beeswax 1 pound; resin, 4 ounces, turpentine 8 ounces, sulphate of copper 8 ounces, arsenic 1 ounce. Mix with heat.

2nd. Yellow wax 1 pound, burgundy pitch 6 oz, turpentine 4 oz, powdered verdigris 2 ounces. Mix with heat, then spread the composition on linen or leather, and polish the surface. Cut it into small pieces.

CORN SOLVENT.—Potash 2 parts, salt sorrel 1 part. Mix in fine powder, lay a small quantity on the corn for four or five successive nights, binding it on with rags.

Never cut your corns to remove them, when they become hard, soak them in warm water, and then with a small pumice stone rasp down the corn. Try it and you will never use a knife afterwards.

The green mountain salve refered to in connection with bone spavin treatment, is almost a certain cure for corns.

The Celebrated Three Minute Salve.

1 pound of caustic potash 4 drs; belladonna, 2 ounces pure oxide maganese, mix with 1-2 pint of water. Apply to shaved corn or wart a few minutes, then wash off and soak in sweet-oil.

It is put up in drachm bottles, with showy labels, and retails at 50 cents; wholesales at 25.

To Cure a Wen.

Wash it with common salt dissolved in water, every day, and it will be removed in a short time. Or make a strong brine of alum-salt; simmer it over the fire. When thus prepared wet a piece of cloth in it every day, and apply it constantly for one month, and the protuberance will disappear.

How to Cure Snake Bites or any Kind of Poison.

No family should ever be without hartshorn in the house; for it is the most valuable remedy known for all kinds of poisons: For snake bites take 6 to 8 drops in a little water about every 5 or 10 minutes until relieved; at the same time apply freely to the parts affected until the swelling is all gone. This never fails to cure.

Sea-Sickness Curable.

I am much surpised at the opinion which is prevalent, of the utter incurability of sea-sickness. I believe the opinion to exist among the non-medical part of the community from sheer ignorance, and amongst sea-going surgeons from a supineness in applying remedies—a fault to which they are rather too subject. In the greater number of instances I allow the stomach to discharg its contents once or twice, and then, if there is no organic disease, I give five drops of chloroform in a little water, and if necessary, repeat the dose in four or six hours. The almost constant effect of this treatment, if enjoined with a few simple precautions, is to cause an immediate sensation, as it were, of warmth in the stomach, accompanied by almost total relief of the nausea and sickness, likewise curing the distressing headache, and usually causing a quite sleep, from which the passenger awakes quite well.

Plating and Gilding without a Battery.

Watt's Electro Metallurgy says: A very useful solution of silver or gold for plating or gilding without the aid of a battery may be made as follows: Take, say, 1 ounce of nitrate of silver, dissolved, in 1 quart of distilled or rain water. When thoroughly dissolved, throw in a few crystals of hyposulphite of soda, which will at first form a brown precipitate, but which eventually becomes redissolved if sufficient hyposulphite has been employed. A slight excess of this salt must however, be added. The solution thus formed may be used for coating small articles of steel, brass, or German silver, by simply dipping a sponge in the solution and rubbing it over the surface of the article to be coated. I have succeeded in coating steel very satisfactory by this means, and have found the silver so firmly attached to the steel (when the solution has been carefully made) that it has been removed with considerable difficulty. A solution of gold may be made in the same way, and applied as described. A concentrated solution of either gold or silver thus made, may be used for coating parts of articles which have stripped or blistered, by applying it with a camel hair pencil to the part, and touching the spot at the same time with a thin clean strip of zinc.

Plating on Iron or Steel.

If your inquirer will follow the directions below, he will have no trouble in plating on iron or steel. Take two quarts rain water, dissolve two pounds cyanide of potassium, and filter. This solution is only for steel or iron. In order to plate steel or iron, dip it into pure sulphuric acid for one minute, then clean with pumice stone and brush; rince, and hang in cyanide solution of potassium for three minutes, or until it becomes white; then hang in silver solution until plated heavy enough.

Metal Founders' Blacking.

To provide metal founders with a blacking possessing good sleeking and heat resisting properties, and to enable them to produce castings with smooth skins of desired hues, the inventor mixes sea weed, sea grass, or sea plants, in any convenient or desired proportion, with still coke, peat charcoal, soft wood charcoal, gas coke, coked coal, oil retort coke, coal dust, soot, hard wood charcoal, or other suitable coke or charcoal, or with lime, chalk, or clay, or with a mixture of two or more of these substances. The seaweed may be added in the newly cut, partially dried, or dried and pulverised state to the coke, charcoal, lime, chalk, or clay, the latter being either in a rough or ground condition. The addition of seaweed to coke, charcoal, lime, chalk, and clay in every proportion, so long as the moisture is sufficient to cause the mixed mass to form a paste in the process of reducing or grinding or to cause the particles of the blacking when furnished to adhere and form lumps, is beneficial either, first, for improving the quality, or, second, for reducing the cost.

This is an English invention recently patented by J. C. Sellars, Birkenhead.

Spermaceti Ointment.

Valuable as an Ingredient of the above; also as a Dressing for Blisters or Old Sores, and as a Healing Ointment-

Take 1 ounce of spermaceti, 1 1-2 drachms of white wax, 2 ounces of sweet olive-oil (in very hot weather, 1 3-4 ounces). Melt together over a gentle fire, and stir constantly till cold.

Plaster of Paris.

It is said that the addition of a small quantity of finely pulverised marsh-mallow roots to calcined plaster of Paris will prevent the mass, when mixed with water, from hardening so rapidly as it commonly does, so as to prevent its applicability to many purposes. It will require nearly an hour to become thoroughly set; and then it will be found to have acquired such an extreme toughness and tenacity as to permit it to be filed, turned, and boared, and otherwise manipulated, almost as satisfactorily as ivory, bone, or meerschaum. Mixed with different coloring matters, an excellent imitation of marble can be produced.

CEMENT FOR METAL AND GLASS.—The following cement will firmly attach any metallic substance to glass or porcelain : Mix two ounces of a thick solution of glue with one ounce of linseed oil varnish, or three fourths of an ounce of venice turpentine; boil them together, stirring them until they mix as thoroughly as possible. The pieces cemented should be tied together for two or three days.

DIAMOND CEMENT.—Take isinglass, soak it in water until it becomes soft, then dissolve it in proof-spirit, and add a little resin-varnish. Used for joining china, glass, &c. An excellent and reliable cement.

VERY DURABLE CEMENT FOR IRON AND STONE.—M. Pollack, of Bautzen, saxtony, states that, for a period of several years, he has used, as a cement to fasten stone to stone and iron to iron, a paste made of pure oxide of lead, litharge, and glycerine in a concentrated state. This mixture hardens rapidly, is insoluble in acids, (unless quite concentrated,) and is not affected by heat. M. Pollack has used it to fasten the different portions of a fly-wheel with great success; while, when placed between stones, and once hardened, it is easier to break the stone than the joint.

LIQUID GLUE.—Fill a vessel (i use a glass jar) with broken-up glue of the best quality, then fill it with a acetic acid. Keep it in hot water for a few hours, until the glue is all melted, and you will have an excellent glue always ready.

Cure for Bone Felon.

As soon as you discover that you have a felon forming, get a small fly blister which apply and leave on six or eight hours, or until it blisters. You will then have only a blister to cure, as you will not be troubled further with the felon. We have known this to succeed in numbers of cases, and a great deal of suffering escaped.

HOW TO CURE A FELON.—First apply an ointment of iodide of iron, then on this put a warm poultice made with a strong decoction of sweet-flag root and bread. Renew this often for at least twelve hours, or until the felon is brought to a head. A cure will be effected in from one to three days.

A SURE CURE FOR A FELON.—Apply a poultice of onions; renew every morning, noon, and night, for three or four days. No matter how bad the case, lancing the finger will be unnecessary if this poultice be used. The remedy is sure, safe, and speedy.

Rose-Salve.

For Sore Lips, Chapped Hands; also for softening the Skin and beautifying the Complexion.

Take, of pure white wax, 1 ounce; of fresh olive-oil, 2 3-4 ounces. Melt together, in a glazed earthen cup, over a gentle heat. Place it, in while melting, 1-2 drachm of alkanet-root, previously tied in a coarse and thin muslin bag; observing, frequently, to squeeze out the bag, so that the color may be diffused through the fluid. Do this until a deep-red color is obtained.

When the ointment has been made, and is cooling, add 10 drops of genuine oil of rose, and stir the whole together till it is cold.

For Burns and Scalds.

Take 1 ounce of spermacti ointment, 2 drachms of Goulard's extract (liquor of the subacetate of lead). Thoroughly mix with a wooden spoon. Spread thickly upon lint or linen, and apply to the parts. Renew the application several times a day. This is an invaluable remedy.

A Speedy Cure for Rheumatism.

Dr. R. H. Boyd states that he cures inflammatory rheumatism in from three to seven days by the following method: He gives first a full emetic dose of ant. et potass. tart., and when this has operated, five drops of tinct. opii and five drops tinct. colchici every three or four hours, and a teaspoonful of a half-pint mixture, containing 3 iv. potass. acet. every hour. When the patient becomes very hungry, and is quite free from pain, having fasted several days, he allows two tablespoonfuls of milk or one oyster three times a day, increasing the quantity gradually each day.—Michagan University Medical Journal, May, 1871.

Carnial Neuralgia Relieved by Gelseminum.

Dr. Philip C. Williams states, that in supra-orbital neuralgia, not malarial or dependent upon organic disease, the yellow jessamine affords the utmost relief. He is himself subject to violent attacks, which are always controlled by this remedy, all others having failed, and he has confirmed this experience on a great many others. In neuralgia of the scalp it has the same happy effects; in maxillary and spinal neuralgias it has failed. One dose of 30 to 40 drops of the tincture usually suffices. Sometimes it is repeated after an hour, and the 20 to 30 drop doses every four hours, continued some days, will prevent recurrence.—Baltimore Medical Journal.

Toothache and Neuralgia.

REMEDIES.—As given by Dr. Chase. Best alcohol, 1 oz., laudanum, 1-8 oz., chloroform, liquid, 5-8 oz., gum camphor 1-2 oz., oil of cloves 1-2 oz., sulphuric ether, 3-4 oz., and oil of lavender, 1 dr., if there is a nerve exposed, this will quiet it. Apply with lint. also rub on the gums and upon the face against the tooth freely. No family should ever be without the above in the house, for it never fails to give ease.

MAGNETIC PAIN KILLER AND TOOTHACHE DROPS.—Alcohol 95 per cent, 2 oz laudanum, 1-2 oz gum camphor 2 oz, oil cloves, 2 drs. Mix and color with tinc of red sanders.

Excellent Tooth Paste.

Suds of castile soap and spirits of camphor, of each an equal quantity, thicken with an equal quantity of pulverised chalk and charcoal, to a thick past· Apply it with the finger or brush. Sold for 25 cents a box.

BOILS.—I have recently got rid of eleven or twelve troublesome boils by taking a teaspoonful, in water, of the following mixture, before every meal: 2 grains bicloride of mercury, 2 drachms iodide of potassium, 2 ounces sirup of sarsparilla, 2 ounces water. The boils were gone before I had taken half the medicine.—D. B., of N. Y.

Glycerine and litherage stirred to a paste, hardens rapidly, and makes a suitable cement for iron upon iron, for two stone surfaces, and especially for fastening iron to stone. The cement is insoluble, and is not attacked by strong acids.

FOR DIARRHEA, when accompanied by pain.—Take 2 drachms concentrated sulphuric ether, 2 drachms spirit lavender comp., 1-2 drachm wine of opium, three drops of oil cloves. Mix.
One teaspoonful on a lump of sugar is the dose for an adult. To be shaken before pouring out and eaten quickly. To be repeated every quarter or half hour if the case be severe.

Electric Silver Plating is done Every Way.

The same as gold (using coin,) except that rock salt is used instead of the cyanurt of potassium, to hold the silver in solution for use, and when it is the proper strength of salt, it has a thick curdy appearance, or you can add salt until the silver will deposite an the article to be plated, which is all that is required.
This method entails no trouble with using a battery, and the successful result of a long series of experiments in electroplating.

Silver solution for plating German silver, copper, brass, &c., &c.—Take 3 oz nitric-acid put in a bottle, and add one american 25 cent piece, cut fine, let it dissolve; add 3 oz quick silver; let it dissolve; add 2 qts rain water and it is ready for use.

Directions for use.—Immerse the article to be plated in the solution; let it remain a few minutes. Now rub gently with a piece of sponge, wet with the solution, and polish with buckskin. The thickness of the plate may be increased by repeating.

Liquid Glue or Mucilage.

Fine, clean glue or mucilage; 1lb gumarabic or gumacasia, 10 oz., water 1 qt; melt by heat in a glue kettle or water bath; when entirely melted, add slowly 10 ozs strong nitric acid; set off to cool, and bottle, adding a couple of cloves to each bottle. Sells for 25 cts., per bottle.

To make Bug Poison.

Take 1 pt. of alcohol, 2 oz. of sal ammonial, 1 pt. spirits turpentine, 2 oz. carrosive sublimate, and 2 oz. camphor gum. Dissolve the camphor in the alcohol, then pulverize the carrosine sublimate and sal ammonice and add to it, after which put in spirits turpentine, and shake well together.

This is equal to any Bed Bug exterminator.

Water Proof Oil Blacking.

Camphene, 1 pt., add all the india rubber it will dissolve, currier's oil, 1 pt., tallow, 7 lbs. lampblack, 2 oz., mix thoroughly by heat.

Superior Combined Black Writing and Copying Fluid.

This Fluid is warranted to flow as freely as any now in use, to give a perfect copy, and not to thicken or mould, as it is made from the best of chemicals. The purchaser must not expect to find this fluid jet black when first opened, as its exclusion from the air makes its first appearance pale, but on its exposure to the air in the inkstand or in writing it soon becomes a beautiful jet black. The blotter should not be used when copies are required.

Recipe for making the ink.—Take 2 gallons of rain water,

3-4 pounds of nutgalls, bruised or ground coarse; 1-4 pound gum arabic, best article; 1-4 pound copperas, 1-4 pound coffee sugar, 1-4 ounce cloves. Boil for three hours, then let it stand in kettle or barrel for ten days, stirring it occasionally, when it is ready for use. Before botling add 1 ounce of glycerine to every gallon made. The older it gets the better it is. After being kept one year it is the best writing fluid in use. Cost of manufacturing 40 cents per gallon.
Proved and tested 1868.

Another Copying Ink.—Take any good bodied ink, (not writing fluid), and add to it one fourth of its bulk of glycerin, he will have the article he calls for. The glycerin prevents the drying of the ink, and when he has written a page he can take a copy in the way described. After taking copy, take up any remaining ink with a common blotter, turn over the leaf and go on writing, copying each page as he proceeds. The writer has copied in this way for years with perfect satisfaction. If the ink dries too quick, add more glycerin; if too slowly, use less. It is desirable to write an even hand with no very fine or very heavy strokes, as the fine ones may dry too quick, and the heavy ones may blot in copying.

American Commercial Writing Ink.—Take 1-4 lb. extract of logwood to 1 gal. of clean soft water; heat to a boiling point in a perfectly clean iron kettle, skim well, stir; add 90 gr's. bichromate of potash, 15 gr's. prussiate of potash, dissolved in 1-2 pt. of hot water, then stir for 3 minutes, take off strain.

Fine Indelible Marking Ink.—Nitrate of silver, 100 gr., distilled or soft water, 1 oz. gum arabic, 2 drs. sap green or indigo, 1 scruple, mix. This is the finest quality of marking ink made.

Blue.—Take soft Prussian blue and oxolic acid in equal parts, powder them finely, and then add soft water to bring it to a thin paste. Let stand for a few days, then add soft water to make the desired shade of colors, adding a little gum arabic to prevent its spreading.

RED INK.—An oz. phial put one teaspoonful of aqua ammonia, gum arabic size of two or three peas, and six grains of No. 40 carmine; fill up with soft water, and it is soon ready for use.

A BRIGHT RED INK.—Cochineal 2 oz. brused; pour over it 1 quart of boiling water and let it stand.   Boil 2 oz. brazil wood in one pint soft water for half an hour, and in 24 hours mix, the two together; then disolve 1 2 oz. gum arabic in a pint of hot water, and when cold add to the other, stir well, bottle, let stand one week then strain through muslin.

HOW TO MAKE PRINTING INK.—Pure balsam copaiba, 9 oz., lamp-black, 3 oz., indigo and prussian blue each 5 drs., Indian red, 3 4 oz., yellow soap, 3 oz., mix and grind to the utmost smoothness.

Hair Dye, No. 1.

Crystalized nitrate of silver 1 drachm, soft water 1 oz.

No. 2. Sulpluret of potassium, 1 drachm, soft water 1 oz. Keep in separate bottles.

Directions.—Cleanse the hair well by washing, from grease and oil, then apply Nos. 1, and 2 alternately with different tooth brushes for each number; when dry wash well with soap.

Pearl Drops.

1-2 lb prepared chalk, 1-2 pint bay rum, 10 oz glycerine, 1 oz cologne, 2 quarts of rain water.   This will fill 2 doz, 2 oz bottles, retails for 50 cents per bottle.

The above is one of the best compounds known for removing tan, freckles, bloches, and beautifying the complexion.

MACASSAR OIL—Olive oil, 1 qt., alcohol, 2 1-2 oz., rose oil, 1 1-2 oz., then tie 1 oz., chipped alkanet root in a muslin bag, and put it in the oil; let it alone some days, until it turns the color of a pretty red, then remove to other oils. Do not press it.

NEW YORK BARBERS, STAR HAIR OIL.—Castor oil 6 1-2 pts., alcohol, 1 1-2 pts., citronella and lavender oil, each 1-2 oz. Sold at one dollar per bottle.

OX MORROW.—Melt 4 oz., ox tallow, white wax, 1 oz., fresh lard, 6 oz.; when cold add 1 1-2 oz., oil bergamot.

HAIR RESTORATIVE.—Castor oil, 8 oz., jamaica rum, 8 oz., oil lavenders, 30 drops, oil rose, 10 drops. Shake well and apply freely.

COLONE. A SUPERIOR ARTICLE.—Take 90 per cent. best alcohol, 1 gal, add to it 1 oz., oil of bergamot, 1 oz., orange, 2 drs., of oil cedar, 1 dr., oil of nevol, and 1 dr., oil of rosemary. Mix well and it is fit for use.

COLONE WATER.—Oils rosemary and lemon, each 1-4 oz., oils bergamot and lavender, each 1-2 oz., oil cinnamon, 8 drops; oils cloves and rose, each 15 drops, deadorized alcohol, 2 qts; shake 2 or 3 times a day for a week.

SHAVING CREAM.—White wax, spermacti, and almond oil, each 1-4 oz.; melt, and while warm beat in 2 squares of windsor soap, previously reduced to a paste with rose water.

VARNISH FOR IRON WORK.—To make a good black varnish for iron work, take eight pounds of asphaltum and fuse it in an iron kettle; then add five gallons of boiled linseed oil, one pound of litherago, half a pound of sulphate of zinc (add these slowly, or it will fume over,) and boil them about three hours. Now add one and a half pounds of dark gum amber, and boil for two hours longer, or until the mass will become quite thick when cool, after which it should be thinned with turpentine to due consistency.

CELEBRATED RECIPE FOR SILVER WASH.—One ounce of nitric acid, one ten cent piece, and one ounce of quicksilver. Put in an open glass vessel, and let it stand until dissolved; then add one pint of water, and it is ready for use. Make it into a powder by adding whiting, and it may be used on brass, copper, german silver, etc.

CEMENT FOR AQUARIA.—Many persons have attempted to make aquarium, but have failed on account of the extreme difficulty in making the tank resist the action of water for any length of time. Below is a receipt for a cement that can be relied upon; it is perfectly free from anything that injures the animals or plants; it sticks to glass, metal, wood, stone, etc., and hardens under water. A hundred different experiments with cements have been tried, but there is nothing like it. It is the same as that used in constructing the tanks of the Zoological Gardens, in London, and is almost unknown in this country. One part, by measure, say a gill, of litherage; one gill of plaster of paris; one gill of dry white sand; one-third of a gill of finely-powdered rosin. Sift and keep corked tight until required for use, when it is to be made into a putty by mixing in boiled oil (linseed) with a little patent dryer added. Never use it after it has been mixed (that is, with the oil) over fifteen hours. This cement can be used for marine as well as fresh water aquaria, as it resists the action of salt water. The tank can be used immediately, but it is best to give it three or four hours to dry.

TRANSFERRING ON GLASS.—Colored or plain engravings, photographs, lithographs, water colors, oil colors, craynon, steel plates, newspaper cuts, mezzotinto, pencil, writing, show cards, labels—or in fact anything.

Directions.—Take glass that is perfectly clean—window glass will answer—clean it thoroughly; then varnish it taking care to have it perfectly smooth; place it where it will be entirely free from dust; let it stand over night; then take your engraving, lay it in clear water until it is wet through (say ten or fifteen minutes), then lay it upon a newspaper, that the moisture may dry from the surface, and still keep the side damp. Immediately varnish your glass the second time, then place your engraving on it, pressing it down firmly, so as to exclude every particle of air; next rub the paper from the back, until it is of uniform thickness—so thin that you can see through it, then varnish it the third time, and let it dry.

Materials used for the above art.—Take two ounces balsam of fir, to one ounce of spirits of turpentine; apply with a camel's hair brush.

To Transfer Engravings to Plaster Casts.—Cover the plate with ink, polish its surface in the usual way, then put a wall of paper round; then pour on it some fine paste made with plaster paris. Jerk it to drive out the air bubbles, and let it stand one hour, when you have a fine impression.

Receipt for Making Artificial Honey.—To 10 lbs. sugar add 3 lbs. water, 40 grains cream tartar, 10 drops essence pepermint, and 3 lbs. strained honey. First dissolve the sugar in water and take off the scum; then dissolve the cream of tartar in a little warm water, which you will add with some little stirring; then add the honey; heat to a boiling point, and stir for a few minutes.

Preservation of Meat, Vegatables, &c.

In the Moniteur Scientifique for March, 1871, Dr. G. Declat describes a process of preserving both vegetable and and animal food material, which is said to have been used successfully in Paris. It consists in soaking the substances in aqueous solutions of various strengths of pure carbolic acid, and then drying them.

Darkness in Treatment of Small-Pox.

Mr. J. H. Waters states that if a patient, in the beginning of the attack, be put in a room from which absolutely all light is excluded save that of a candle, the effect is to arrest the disease in the popular or vesicular stage; it never becomes purulent, and the skin between the vesicles is never inflamed or swollen; the liquor sanguinis is prevented from becoming pus; the large scabs of matter never form over the face; there is no intense pain, and only trifling itching, and the smell is either very slight or altogether wanting.—London Lancet.

Preventitive of Sea-Sickness.

Boil two ounces of opium, two drachms extract of henbane, ten grains of mace, and two ounces of soap, in three pints of water, for half an hour. When cold, add one quart of rectified spirits and three drachms of spirits of ammonia. To be used as an embroeation.

Cure for the Love of Strong Drink.

Tartar emetic, 9 grains; rose water, 4 oz. Mix. Put a table-spoonful into the whole quantity the person drinks through the day. Be sure not to exceed this quantity.

Receipt for Manufacturing American Champagne.

For ten gallons of water take one and one-half pint of brewer's yeast, one-half pound of tartaric acid, (or quantity to suit taste,) and five pounds of common coarse brown sugar. Make the water milk warm, put in the yeast first; ten minutes after put in the tartaric acid and sugar; then let it cool, stirring it occasionally through the day. Bottle at night, after it has settled. You can color and improve it by adding a little sherry or St. Julian. By using white sugar it is almost impossible to tell it from real champagne. Cost of manufacture 20 cents per gallon.

Blackberry Wine.

There is no wine equal to blackberry wine when properly made, in flavor or for medicinal purposes, and all persons who can conveniently do so, should manufacture enough for their own use every year, as it is invaluable in sickness as a tonic, and nothing is better for the bowel complaint. We therefore give the receipt for making it: Measure your berries and bruise them; to every gallon add one quart of boiling water. Let the mixture stand twenty-four hours, stirring occasionally; strain off the liquor into a cask; to every gallon add two pounds of sugar; cork it tight and let stand till the following October, and you will have wine ready for use without further labor, that every family might highly appreciate and never do without afterward if they can help it.

Fixing Lead Pencil Marks on Paper.

Stretch the drawing tightly on a board, with drawing pins, and pour a little pure milk (if it can be obtained) on the paper, turning the board about till the milk has flowed all over the drawing. The turning must be done at once as the milk must not be allowed to stand on the paper. When the whole surface is wetted, let the milk drain off, and leave the board with the drawing in the air to dry.

The Hair and Whiskers.

HAIR RESTORERS AND INVIGORATORS.—There are hundreds, Lyon's Wood's, Barry's, Bogle's, Jane's, Storr's, Baker's, Drisco's, Phalon's, Haskel's, Allen's, Spalding's, etc. But, though all under different names, are similar in principle; being vegetable oils dissolved in alcohol, with the addition of spirit of soap, and an astringent material, such as tincture of catechu, or infusion of bark. The best is to dissolve one ounce of castor oil in one quart of 95 alcohol, and add one ounce of the tincture of cantharades, two ounces of the tincture of catechu, two ounces of lemon juice, two ounces of the tincture of cinchona; and to scent it, add the oil of cinnamon, or oil of rosmary, or both.

To CURE BALDNESS.—Take water, one pint; pearl-ash, one-half ounce; onion juice, one gill. Mix, and cork in a bottle. Rub the head night and morning, with a rough towel, dipped in the mixture.

To MAKE THE HAIR SOFT AND GLOSSY.—Put one ounce of castor oil in one pint of bay rum or alcohol, and color it with a little of the tincture of alkanet root. Apply a little every morning.

POUDRE SUBTILE FOR REMOVING SUPERFLUOUS HAIR.—Take powdered quick-lime, two parts; sulphuret of arsenic, one part; starch, one part; mix into a fine powder, and keep in a close corked bottle. When required for use, take a small quantity and add two or three drops of water, and apply on the part you desire to remove the hair from—let it remain about one minute, or until it becomes red, then wash off.

OIL TO MAKE THE HAIR GROW.—Olive Oil one qr. pt., Add oils of Rosmary and Origanum, each one sixth oz. Apply freely.

WHISKERS OR MOUSTACHE FORCED TO GROW.—Cologne, two ounces, liquid hartshorn, one drachm; tincture cantharides, two drachms; oil rosemary, twelve drops; oil nutmeg, twelve drops; and lavender, twelve drops. This is the recipt used in making the celebrated GRAHAM ONGENT.

DIRECTIONS TO COLOR THE HAIR.—First wash the head, beard, or moustaches, with soap and water; afterwards with clean water. Dry, and apply the gallic acid solution, with a clean brush. When it is almost dry, take a small tooth comb, and with a fine brush, put on the teeth of the comb a little of the silver solution, and comb it through the hair, when it becomes a brilliant jet black. Wait for a few hours; then wash the head again with clean water. If you want to make a brown dye, add double or treble the amount of water to the silver solution, and you can obtain any shade or color you choose.

BALM OF BEAUTY.—Pure soft water, one qt., pulverized castile soap, four oz., emulsion of bitter almonds, six oz., tincture of benzoin, two drs., rose and orange flower water, each, eight oz., borax one dr; add five grs., of bichloride of mercury to every eight ounces of the mixture. To use, apply a cotton or linen cloth to the face, etc. This is a reliable article and gives the manufacturer a large profit.

New Method of Bleaching or Disinfecting Feathers.

Clean the feathers first from greasy matter, and then place them for three hours in a dilute solution of bichromate of potassa, to which a small quantity of nitric acid has been added. The feathers will become greenish from a deposit of chromic sesqui-oxide, which is removed by weak sulphurous acid, when the feathers are left perfectly white. The nascent oxygen developed in the reduction of the chromic acid to the oxide is, of course, the bleaching agent, and so powerful is it that the darkest feathers will become perfectly white.

CHOW-CHOW.—Take quarter peck green tomatoes, same quantity, each of pickling beans and white onions, one dozen each cucumbers and green peppers; one head of cabbage. Season with mustard, celery seed, and salt to the taste. Pour over these the best cider vinegar sufficient to cover; boil slowly for two hours, continually stirring, and add, while hot, two table-spoonfuls of the finest salad oil.

Recipes for Dyeing Carpet Warp.

It should be borne in mind that the material when wet always looks darker than it will when dry, and in order to judge whether the desired shade is obtained, it is necessary to ring out a small portion quite dry before deciding that the shade is deep enough. After the material is dried it should be thoroughly rinsed in an abundance of soft water until no more color is imparted to the water.

GREEN.—For three pounds of warp, take one pound of fustic, one-half pound of logwood chips, a piece of blue vitriol the size of a hickory nut, and three pails of water. Boil one hour.

PURPLE.—For fifteen pounds of warp, take four pound of logwood chips; boil them in two pails of water. Dissolve one pound of alum in a pail of hot water; pour the alum water into that containing the logwood, and boil your cotton in it one hour.

YELLOW.—For five pounds of cotton, dissolve eight ounces sugar of lead in four quarts of warm water, and dissolve five ounces bicromate of potash in three quarts of warm water. Put the cotton in the lead water first; wring it out and put it in the bichromate of potash water; continue until you have the shade you wish.

PINK.—For five pounds of cotton, take two pounds of Nicauragua or red wood, four of solution of tin; boil the wood an hour in six quarts of water. Pour the dye into a tub and ad the solution of tin; put in the cotton; let it stand five minutes, and you will have a nice color. [The solution of tin may be had of the druggists, under the name of the chloride or muriate of tin.]

To DYE WOOLENS, RED, CRIMSON, AND SCARLET.—Coarse woolen stuffs are dyed red with madder or archil, but fine cloth is almost exclusively dyed with cochineal, though the color which it recieves from kermes is much more durable. Brazil-wood is scarcely used, except as an auxiliary, because the color which it imparts to wool is not permanent.

RED DYES.—The coloring matter employed for dyeing red are archil, madder, carthamus, kermes, cochineal, and brazil-wood.

COCOA-NUT CAKE.—Take one-half cup of butter, two cups of sugar, three eggs, one cup of milk (sweet,) three and one-half cups of flour, one tea-spoonful of baking-powder, one coca-nut, grated fine. Beat the eggs and sugar together, then add the flour and milk; lastly add the cocoa-nut. Mix well, and pour into a pan for the oven.

GREEN CORN PUDDING.—Take twelve ears of corn, split the rows in the centre, then scrape out the pulp with a knife; this will leave the hull on the cob. Add four eggs, one pint milk, one spoonful butter, sweeten and flavor to taste. Bake one-half hour.

FAVORITE CAKE.—Three cups sugar, two cups butter, five cups flour, one pound fruit, one cup milk, five eggs, one tea-spoon soda.

GERMAN PUFFS.—One quart of milk, six eggs, sixteen ta-blespoonfuls of flour, and a little salt. Bake in small tins.

TO MAKE FINE ROLLS.—Warm a bit of butter in half a pint of milk; add two spoonful of small beer yeast and some salt ; with these ingredients mix two pounds of flour; let it rise one hour, and kneed it well; form the rolls, and bake them in a quick oven twenty minutes.

COCOA-NUT PIE.—Cut off the brown part of the cocoa-nut, grate the white part, and mix it with milk, and set it on the fire and boil it slowly eight or ten minutes. To a pound of cocoa-nut allow a quart of milk, eight eggs, four tablespoon-fuls of sifted white sugar, a glass of wine, a small cracker pounded fine, two spoonfuls of melted butter, and half a nut-meg. The eggs and sugar should be beaten together to a froth, then the wine stirred in. Put them into the milk and cocoa-nut, which should be first allowed to get quite cool; add the cracker and nutmeg, turn the whole into deep pie-plates, with a lining and rim of puff-paste. Bake them as soon as turned into the plates.

STEAM PUDDING.—One quart flour, one coffee cup chopped raisins or currants, one teacup chopped suet, one teacup half filled with molasses, finish with brown sugar, one teaspoon soda, two teacups sweet milk, a little salt. Mix, and steam three hours. Sauce.

SPONGE GINGERBREAD.—Two pound of flour, one of sugar, one of butter, six eggs, one pint of molasses, one pint of milk, two tablespoonful of ginger, one of cinnamon, one of cloves, two of pearlash.

TO MAKE RUSK.—One cup butter, one cup sugar, one pound of flour, one pint of milk, three eggs, one cup of yeast, one teaspoonful of saleratus. Bake in a quick oven.

EXCELLENT BISCUITS.—Take of flour, two pounds; carbonate of amonia, three drachms in fine powder; white sugar, four ounces; arrowroot, one ounce; butter; four ounces; one egg. Mix into a stiff paste with new milk, and beat them well with a rolling pin for half an hour, roll out thin, and cut them out with a docker, and bake in a quick oven for fifteen minutes.

OMLETTE SOUFFLE.—Beat the whites of ten eggs to a stiff froth, the yolks with three quarters of a pound of white sugar, juice and rind of one lemon; mix all together lightly. Butter a dish that will just hold it, and bake ten or fifteen minutes.

PRESERVATION OF EGGS.—Eggs may be preserved for any length of time by excluding them from the air. One of the cleanest and easiest modes of doing this is to pack them in clean, dry salt, in barrels or tubs, and to place them in a cool and dry situation. An old shipmaster says he has eaten eggs thus preserved that were a year old, and that had been some months aboard ship, in a tropical climate, and yet retained all the peculiar sweetness of newly-laid eggs. Some persons place eggs which they wish to preserve in a netting, or on a sieve or cullender, and immerse them for an instant in a cauldron of boiling water, befor packing them away. Sometimes eggs are placed in vessels containing milk of lime, or strong brine, or rubbed over with butter, lard, or gum water; all of which act by excluding the air.

BUTTER, HOW TO KEEP.—Butter can be kept sweet and nice for a whole year by working into it a very little powdered loaf-sugar and powdered saltpeter; put into a jar or tub, make a brine with salt as strong as water will dissolve and completely cover the butter with this; then make a small muslin bag and fill with salt and put in. Care must be taken that the butter is always covered with the brine.

To KEEP EGGS.—Add to four quarts of air-slacked lime two tablespoonfuls of cream tartar, two of salt, and four quarts cold water. Put fresh eggs into a stone jar, and pour this mixture over them. This will keep nine dozen, and if fresh when laid down, they will keep many months. If the water settles away so as to leave the upper layer uncovered, add more water. Cover close, and keep in a cool place.

CHEAP WHITE HOUSE PAINT.—Take skim milk, two quarts; eight ounces fresh slacked lime, six ounces linseed oil, two ounces white burgundy pitch, three pounds spanish white. Slack the lime in water, expose to the air, and mix in about one quarter the milk; the oil, in which the pitch is previously dissolved, to be added, a little at a time; then the rest of the milk, and afterwards the spanish white. This quantity is sufficient for thirty square yards, two coats, and costs but a few cents. If the other colors are wanted, use, instead of spanish white, other coloring matter.

How to make a Valuable Washing Compound.

Take one pound of Babbit soap, slice it up finely, and dissolve it in two quarts of boiling soft water. Then in another dish, take ten ounces of sal soda, six ounces good white unslacked lime, soft boiling water two quarts, and two ounces of borax. Mix well, then let stand and settle, after which pour off the clear water or solution into the dish containing the soap, which should be kept hot; then stir well and add one half-ounce of aqua amonia, and one half ounce of benzine; mix all together thoroughly and set away to cool, and you have the best compound in the world.

Directions for using.—Put on your water and let it warm, then put in one pound of the compound, to every three gallons of water. Put in your white clothes and let them boil

very briskly from ten to twenty minutes, according to degree
of dirtiness.

Rinse in two waters, blue and hang out. Put your colored
clothes in the same suds and let them boil very slow, eight or
ten minutes, rinse thoroughly and hang out . Then set your
boiler on top of the stove and put in your woolens, not allowing them to boil, but keep in the hot suds five or ten minutes.
Take the suds and mop your floor. Throw a little water on
your white clothes over night, or let them soak in warm
compound suds an hour or so before boiling. Don't crowd
your boiler too full or put in clothes twisted hard from wring-
ing.

FRICTION SOAP.—Take five pounds of brown soap, and ten
pounds of fine sand. Heat them well together over a slow
fire, add whatever kind of scent or coloring you desire, and
while it is yet warm, make it into one-quarter pound cakes,
and it will readily sell at ten cents a cake. It is an excellent
thing for the toilet, and all kinds of washing, clothes ex-
cepted. It will cure skin diseases of every description.

ERASIVE SOAP.—This receipt alone is worth Ten Dollars to
any family; it costs but little to try it. Aquæ amonia, two
ounces; white shaving soap, one ounce; saltpetre, one teaspoonful; soft water, one quart.

CHEMICAL SOFT SOAP.—Take grease eight pounds, sal soda
one pound; melt the grease in a kettle, melt the sodas in soft
water, four gallons, and pour all into a barrel holding forty
gallons, and fill with soft water, and the labor is done.
When the caustic soap cannot be obtained of soap-makers,
you will make it by taking soda-ash and fresh slacked lime,
of each eight pounds; dissolve them in the water with sal
soda, and when settled, pour off the clear liquid as in the
"White Hard Soap with Tallow."

SODA ASH SOAP.—Take of soda ash, two and one-fourth
pounds; unslacked lime, one and one-half pounds; rain water,
six gallons; boil one hour, then set off to settle. Pour off the
clean liquor, and add to it six pounds of clear grease, and
boil till, when cold, it is hard. This will take about two
hours.

To Make Washing Fluid.—To one gallon of soft soap (such as is made by the usual method of boiling the lye of wood ashes and fat together), take four ounces of sal soda, half a gallon of rain or soft water, and one-half gill of spirits of turpentine. Place them all in a pot over the fire, and allow the mixture to boil a few minutes. It is then ready for use, and can be kept in an earthen or stone ware vessel. In using this fluid, the clothes intended to be washed should be soaked ten or twelve hours—say over night—and then to a ten or twelve gallon boiler, or kettle full of clothes, covered with water, add one pint of fluid; boil briskly for fifteen minutes, and then rinse them in fresh water. It will be found that little or no rubbing, of any account, will be found necesary

Silver Soap for Cleaning Silver and Brittannia.—One half pound of soap, three tablespoonfuls of sprits of turpentine, and half a tumbler of water. Let it boil ten minutes; and add six tablespoonfulls of spirits of hartshorn. Make sudds of this and wash with it.

To Make a good Washing Soap without Lie or Greece. —One pound of yellow bar soap; Babbitts is the best; one pound of sal soda, one ounce of borax, four pounds of soft water. Mix all together and boil fifteen minutes. It will make four pounds of soap when cold. Spread the soap on the dirty streaks in your clothing and put them to soak in a tub of water over night and you will save half the labor in washing.

Vinegar from Acetic Acid and Molasses.—Acetic acid, four pounds; molasses, one gallon, put them into a forty gallon cask, and fill it up with rain water; shake it up and let it stand, from one to three weeks, and the result is good vinegar. If this does not make it as sharp as you like, add a little more molasses. But some will object to this because an acid is used: let me say to such, that acetic acid is concentrated vinegar. Take one pound or one pint, or any other quantity of this acid, and add seven times as much soft water, and you have just as good vinegar as can be made from cider, and that instantaneously.

How four pounds of Butter is Made from one gallon of Sweet Milk.—Take one gallon of sweet milk, warm and curdle as you would if you were going to make cheese, (beefs runnet is most commonly used for the purpose) then empty into a common churn, and add eight pounds of butter churn all together for five or ten minutes, then empty out out into a large bowl and work out the whey and color with a little Annetta; now make into rolls and weigh, and you find you have twelve pounds of butter instead of eight pounds, but you have no buttermilk. I have known persons to make butter as above and sell in the markets at first class prices without detection in cool weather, but it does not do well in warm weather. I do not recommend the above, but give it from the fact that there are persons going about through the country selling receipts from five to ten dollars to make four pounds pounds of butter from one gallon of sweet milk.

Liquid Blueing for Clothes—Take best Prussian blue, pulverized, one ounce; oxalic acid, also pulverized, ene-half ounce; soft water; one quart; mix. The acid dissolves the blue and holds it evenly in the water, so that specking will never take place. One or two tablespoonfuls of it is sufficient for a tub of water, according to the size of the wash. This is far prefferable to the blueing sold at stores, and is much cheaper.

Breaking Horses. There is nothing more unreasanable or unwise—we are almost tempted to say inhuman—than the old method of treating horses—namely, allowing them to run wild until a certain age, and then having a violent conflict with them for the mastery. On this subject a well known horsman offers the following sensible remarks:

"I am glad to see that the practice of breaking horses is growing into disuse. Gentle your horses and acquaint them with the duties which they shall have to perform, but never whip them. Accustom them, from their earliest colthood, to be handled; pet them until they enjoy your society; in fact, win their love by kindness. Let them learn what a halter is in a manner which will not shock or frighten them. Teach them to put up with straps and buckles, and, when old enough, have them daily bear or drag some light load; but do it all kindly, and gradually lead them on in their education, so that when the proper time comes, they can be saddled or harnessed with neither risk nor trouble. But to throw the whole burden of a three years' education upon them in about the same number of days, and to conqure the poor, trembling animals by brute force, is it human and unreasonabl. Let us learn and teach our children to treat the animals given us for our service by our Master, in a manner worthy of human beings."

To Remove Bone Spavain from Horses witout Fail.

One ounce of oil vitriol, two ounce of oil spike, two ounces spirits turpentine. Mix all the above in an earthen dish, then add one ounce of oil vitriol. Great care should be taken to fasten the bottle of vitriol to a stick three or four feet long to prevent your getting burnt, as the ingredients will ignite and burn awhile when the vitriol is added.

Directions for Use.—First apply once a day for three days, then let rest three days, then grease well. Be careful and not let it get wet before it is well greased. Then wash with castile soap and apply again as above. Continue the process according to directions until lameness is removed. I could give several other remedies but it not necessary as the above never fails to cure.

Perhaps you might prefer the following $300 receipt: Corrosive sublimate quicksilver; and iodine, each one ounce; with lard only sufficient for a paste.

Directions.—Rub the quicksilver and iodine together, then add the sublime and finally the lard, rubbing thoroughly. Shave off the hair the size of the bone enlargement, then grease all around it, but not where the hair is shaved off, this prevents the action of the medicine, only upon the spavin; now rub in as much of the paste as will lie on a five cent piece only, each morning for four mornings only. In seven or eight days the whole spavin will come out then wash out the wound with suds, soaking well for an hour or two, which removes the poisonous effects of the medicine and faciltates the healing, which will be done by any of the healing salves.

I would use the Green Mountain Salve, which is made as follows : Rosin five pounds, burgundy pitch, bees wax, and mutton tallow, each one quarter of a pound, oil of hemlock, balsam of fir, oil of origanum, oil of red cedar, and venice turpentine, each one ounce; melt the first articles together, then add the oils, and put it in with the other aticles, stirring well, then pour in the cold water and work as wax until cool enough to roll. This salve has no equal for rheumatic pains, or weakness in the side, back, shoulders, or any place where pain may locate itself. When the skin is broken, as in ulcers and bruises, I use it without the verdigris, making a white salve.

ANOTHER SPAVIN CURE.—Take equal parts of oil spike, oil of amber and spirits of turpentine, warm the compound on the stove, being careful that the fire does not get to it, and apply as warm as you can to the spavin, by pouring it on and rubbing it in well with the ball of your thumb, having first shaved the hair off the spavin. Repeat twice per day for two days, when if well rubbed, it will become a running sore. Then wet a sponge with the compound, and apply it twice per day for three days, then stop for three days, and if the spavin has not disappeared, repeat the dose for three days longer. Let the sore heal, then wash it with suds from castile soap, and the spavin will disappear.

To Cure Poll Evil and Fistula.

Take an herb commonly know as sheep sorrell, which grows most everywhere and mash it up, either the root or herb itself and put in water and boil down to a strong thick tea. Take some of the same and put in a puter dish; set it in the sun until it evaporates and thickens about as thick molasses. Wash twice per day with the tea, and apply after each bathing the thickened tea as you would salve. This never fail to effect a permanent cure.

ANOTHER CURE FOR FISTULA.—Open the sore with a knife, then roll thirty grains of arsenic up in a small piece of paper, an press it down in the cut; and let it remain there 18 days; then pare out all dead flesh, wash it with soap every day. Heal it up with rosin and muton tallow in equal portions.

CORNS IN HORSES, HOW TO TREAT.—Cut out the stain, if a suppurating corn, place the foot in a poultice after having opened the abscess; the horn being softened, cut away all the sole which has been released by the pus from its attachment to the secreting surface; tack on an old shoe, and dress with the solution of chloride of zinc one grain, to the ounce of water; afterward shoe with leather and employ stopping to render the horn plastic.

HOW TO TREAT COUGHS IN HORSES.—Crush the oats, damp the hay, give gruel or flax seed tea for drink, clothe warmly, and give three times a day half a pint of the following mixture in a tumblerful of water; extract belladonna one drachm, rubbed down gradually in a pint of cold water until dissolved, then add tincture of squills ten ounces, tincture of ipecac eight ounces.

RING-BONE, ITS TREATMENT.—In the first stages, apply poultices with one drachm each camphor and powered opium; afterward rub with an ointment of iodine and lead one ounce, simple ointment eight ounces (well mixed;) continue the treatment two weeks after all active symptoms have subsided; allow liberal food and rest.

HIDE-BOUND, HOW TREATED.—Plenty of food, clean, soft bedding, healthy exercise, and good grooming; administer daily two drinks, composed of liquor arsenicalis half ounce, tincture muriate iron one ounce, water one pint; mix, and give at one dose.

REMEDY FOR SORE TONGUE IN HORSES.—Take one part sugar of lead, one part bole amonia, and two parts burnt alum, the whole to be added to three quarts of vinegar. With this wash out the mouth twice a day.

REMEDY FOR STRAIN IN HORSES.—Take whisky, one half pint; camphor, one ounce; sharp vinegar, one pint. Mix. Use for bathing.

SLOBBERS IN HORSES.—An infallible, simple, and cheap remedy is a dose or two of from one to two gallons of wheat bran.

GENERAL INFLAMATION OF THE EYE.—Introduce into the eye, two or three times a day, the following lotion: Extract goulard, two drachms, spiritous tincture digitalis, two drachms; tincture opium, two drachms; water, one pint. Two or three drops at a time will suffice.

CRAMP in horses arises from irregular action of the motor nerves. Rubbing the affected parts with a wisp of hay for ten minutes would be beneficial; and should friction alone not remove the tendency to cramp, the parts affected should be rubbed occasionally with a solution of camphor and olive oil.

TO KEEP FLIES FROM HORSES.—Take of green leaves of the shagbark hickory, (Carya Alba) quantum suff.; bruise in hot water, let cool, and strain, and sponge the most exposed parts before the horse leaves the stable. I have found this perfectly effectual in preventing horse flies, common flies, greenheads, and musquetoes from troubling horses, for three or four hours after application.

FOR DISTEMPER.—Bleed in the neck vein, taking about three pints of blood, then give the following: Take one tablespoonful of gunpowder, one of hogs lard, one of soft soap, two of tar, and one of pulverized gum myrrh. Mix thorougly. Put a spoonful of this down his throat as far as you can reach with a paddle or spoon, twice a day. The object is not so much to have him swallow it as it is to have it lodge about the glands of the throat. No danger is to be apprehended from using it freely.

COROSIVE LINIMENT.—Take half a pint of turpentine, one ounce of finely powdered corosive sublimate, one ounce gum camphor; shake well, and let stand twenty-four hours, when it will be ready for use. This liniment will cure big-head and big-jaw, grease, thrush, scratches, swelled legs, hoof rot, foot evil, corns, ulceration of the foot, fistula, poll evil, ringbone, and spavin, in their first stages.

CURE FOR COLIC IN HORSES.—We have found the following receipt very effectual in curing colic: Take as much bread soda as will dissolve in a pint of water—say a teacupfull; put in a strong bottle with a long neck; pour in the water, warm water is best, shake well, and add one ounce of laudanum, one ounce essence ginger, and one ounce chloroform; shake well and drench. The soda alone is very good. Colic is produced by acidity and distension of the bowels. This distension in one place causes contraction in another and entirely locks up the bowels. You want to administer a remedy that will correct the acidity and relax the bowels. Nothing is better, we think, than the above combination, and we would advise all persons who have horses to keep a bottle on hand ready for use. This is also a sure remedy for bots.

SCRATCHES IN HORSES.—Mix white lead and linseed oil in such proportions as will render the application convenient, and I never have known more than two or three applications necessary to effect a cure.

Receipts for the Cure of Diseases in Horses.

The following are receipts that I have obtained from an old English gentleman at a cost of $100.

For Big Head or Jaw.—Take half a pint of turpentine, one ounce of camphor, one ounce of sublimate; mix and let stand for a day and it is fit for use. Use about one table-spoonful on each side of the head or jaw; bathe the parts well with a hot iron. Do this once a day until you use all the medicine, and at the same time commence giving sulphur, about one fourth of a pound to a dose, until you give two or three pounds; do this every four or five days; bleed moderately every sixth day for five or six times, and keep your horse out of wet weather while doctoring him. This medicine is poison.

For Poll Evil—Use about the same quantity of the same medicine, always washing the sore well, if broke, with warm water and soap. Before applying the medicine bleed some three or four times, and give some three or four doses of sulphur, always bathing it with a hot iron.

For Bone, Bog, or Blood Spavin—Make use of the same receipt and same quantity. Omit the sulphur and bleeding, but bathe well, especially for bone spavin.

For Foot Evil—You will use the same medicine, omitting the bathing; keep them out of wet weather or dew, and give three or four doses of sulphur, and bleed two or three times.

For Ring Bone—Use the same medicine and bathe the part well, omitting the sulphur and bleeding.

For Splint Saddle Galls or any hard bony substance, arising from kicks, blows, or sprains, use the same medicine, omitting the bleeding and sulphur, but bathe well.

For Big Shoulder—Take one pint of French brandy and as much aquefortice, as will make it sour so as to bite the tongue, then add one ounce of blue stone, one ounce of corosive sublimate, one ounce of camphor, two vials of oil of spike, one and a half gill of turpentine. Mix them all together, and take a hair brush and rub it in, do this three or four times, always bathing it well with a hot iron, do this every other day; bleed two or three times and give three or four doses of sulphur; and keep them out of bad weather.

For Weak or Inflamed Eyes—Take ten grains of calomel, two grains of red precipitate; mix it well and add to this quantity one teaspoonfull of fresh butter. Mix it well and put a small quantity in the eye with a feather once a day, using a wash at the same time, made by adding one half once of lodanum to one pint of water. Bleed some two or three times in eight or ten days.

For Fistula—Take one pint of strong spirits and as much soap as will dissolve in it while boiling. As soon as it boils pour it on the sore, do this for four mornings. Bleed the 1st, 5th, and 10th morning; or else take one pint of turpentine, one vial of oil of spike, mix this and let it boil and pour it on the sore; use this quantity three mornings in succession and bleed as above directed.

For Founder—As quick as you find your horse is foundered, bleed him in the neck in proportion to the greatness of the founder, then draw his head up and give him one pint of salt added to one quart of water strained, then wet the edge of his hoofs with turpentine.

For Glanders—Make a strong decoction of tobacco boiled, weaken it according to the symptoms, add one-third pint of this to one pint of water and give the quantity every third day. Give your horse a quarter pound of sulphur every fourth or fifth morning until you use two or three pounds. Bleed once a week for three or four weeks, at the same time make a week tea of burdock, yellow poplar and sassaparilla, and let them be his constant drink.

For Botts—Take one pint of new milk, one pint of molasses, and drench your horse. In some twenty minutes give your horse one quart of sage tea as warm as he can drink it, in two or three hours give your horse one pint of linseed oil.

For Colic—In the first place you will bleed your horse freely, then get one half ounce of lodanum, one gill of whisky, three spoonfuls of turpentine, put them in a pint bottle and fill it with warm water and then drench your horse.

For Stifle—Take one half pound shomake bark, one half pound white oak bark, boil in two gallons of water down to two pints, bathe with the ooze twice a day for four days, then make a salve of the white of an egg and an ounce of rosin. Bathe in with a hot iron twice a week for two weeks.

For Hooks—Give half a pound of salts daily for three or four days. Bleed three or four times lightly in eigth or ten days. Rest your horse and feed no corn.

FOUNDER IN HORSES. I send you a receipt for founder in horses. It is a sure and speedy remedy. Take a spoonful of pulverized alum, pull the horses tongue out of his mouth as far as possible, and throw the alum down his throat; let go of his tongue and hold up his head until he swallows. In six hours time no matter how bad the founder, he will be fit for moderate service. I have seen this remedy tested so often with perfect success, that I would not make five dollars difference in a horse foundered if done recently and one that was not.

To GET HORSES OUT OF A FIRE.—A gentleman whose horses had been in great peril by fire, having in vain tried to save them, hit upon the experiment of having them harnessed, as though they were going to their usual work, when; to his astonishment, they were led from the stable without difficulty. The plan of covering their eyes with a blanket does not always succeed.

The End of the Horse.

When the horse falls, he is bled, and his blood is preserved for the use of the dyer. The mane and tail are next cut off for the manufacture of sieves, hair cloths, and bow strings for the violin; the shoes are taken off for the nailer; the hoofs are cut off for combs and various other kinds of horn-work, and a portion of the feet goes to the glue-maker; the skin is stripped off for the tanner, who converts it into excellent leather for boots, harness, etc., and the collar maker finds it, in its rough state, the best material for cart harness. The flesh is then cut up for carniverous beasts in menageries, or for dogs, and, though without knowing that they are hippophagi, (a club of horse-eaters, who regularly advertise their club days,) some of our fellow citizens are regaled in the cheap eating houses of great cities with delicate bits of carcass in the form of pates, pretended beef-steaks or soup. When the flesh and fat have been removed, the stomache and intestines are laid aside for machine straps and strings for musical instruments, and are often sold, for the last purpose, as the best Naples cords; the ribs are turned into buttons and children's toys; the large bones are used for tweezers, whistles, ferules, knife handles, cups and balls, dominoes, etc.; the large, flat bones are of use to the toy men for many things; even the teeth are useful, when polished, to the dentist, and for many purposes for which ivory is required. The bones of the head are either consumed in heating furnaces or crushed for manure. The remainder of the carcass is burnt, and by this process produces ivory-black, soot-black, and valuable manure. And from the fat is extracted a course oil which is used by mechanics.

How to Cure Hog Cholera.

Nearly everybody has a remedy for hog cholera but very few remedies are successful; as a general thing a great deal depends on how hogs are fed. I am informed by an old farmer, who has been very succesful in raising hogs and that he finds that the best thing to prevent it, is by keeping in the pen, where the hogs can run to and eat of, a box or trough of mixture made as follows: Three bushels of slacked ashes, one bushel of lime, one peck of salt; mix all well together. The above mixture should be kept in the pen so that the hogs may run to it any time. I do not think you will ever be bothered with worms in you hogs or hog cholera. Soft soap and soda, mix and give to hogs when sick with cholera; it never fails to cure. A gentleman informs us that he has cured more hogs with the above, when they were so sick that they could not eat anything, and he had to catch them and pour it down their throat.

To Cure Blind Staggers in Hogs.—Put about a spoonful of coal oil in the hogs ears two days in succession; and, also, put a little coal oil on its head, and it will be all right in a short time.

Miscellaneous Receipts.

Preservation of Milk and Cream.—Put the milk into bottles, then place them into a sauce pan with cold water, and gradually raise to a boiling point; take it from the fire, and instantly cork the bottles, then raise the milk once more to the boiling point for half a minute. Finally let the bottles cool in the water in which they were boiled. Milk thus treated will remain perfectly good for six months. Emmigrants, especially those having children, will find the above hint add much to their comfort during their voyage.

How I Make Cider Vinegar.—I put my cider in barrels and let it work until it becomes thoroughly hard. Then, immediately after the new of the moon, I empty my barrels into tubs and let the cider settle, rinsing out my barrels clean. When the sediment has sufficiently settled I put the clear cider back into the barrels. If any mother had been formed, this is also put back. If there is no mother, in order to to cause it to form; I roll up a piece of writing paper and put this into the barrel. I then add to each barrel three gallons of clear rain water, sweetened somewhat sweeter than sugar water, and the bung holes left open.

To Patrons.

In conclusion, I desire to impress upon the minds of the public, the importance and value of this work by earnestly requesting that its pages may be carefully perused, and the receipts as given, farely tested by every family; it gives all the most reliable household remedies, remedies that no family should be without; by its instruction all may become their own physician to a certain extent; the remedies that I have given for all the complaints which every family is subject to, are invaluable, and no household should ever be found without them, for by their presence a good deal of suffering and many a dollar can be saved, and some times life, especially in such cases as Cholera, Cholera Infantum, Croup, etc. Also my treaties on the horse and his diseases, will be invaluable to all who deal in or handle horses. This I know from practical experience. I give several receipts that are worth from ten to fifty times the worth of this book, which will be acknowledged by all who will test their merits; by so doing the value of this small work may be fully appreciated.

To such persons as may desire to engage in the sale of this work, either male or female, I offer very liberal inducements. Special terms furnished on application. Agents wanted in every town and county in the United States. This work will be mailed free to any address on receipt of price, One Dollar.

Address

· T. J. CHRISTY, Olney Ill.

www.ingramcontent.com/pod-product-compliance
Lightning Source LLC
Chambersburg PA
CBHW022037080426
42733CB00007B/876